Editor
Mary S. Jones, M.A.

Editor in Chief
Karen J. Goldfluss, M.S. Ed.

Cover Artist
Barb Lorseyedi

Imaging
James Edward Grace
Craig Gunnell

Publisher

Mary D. Smith, M.S. Ed.

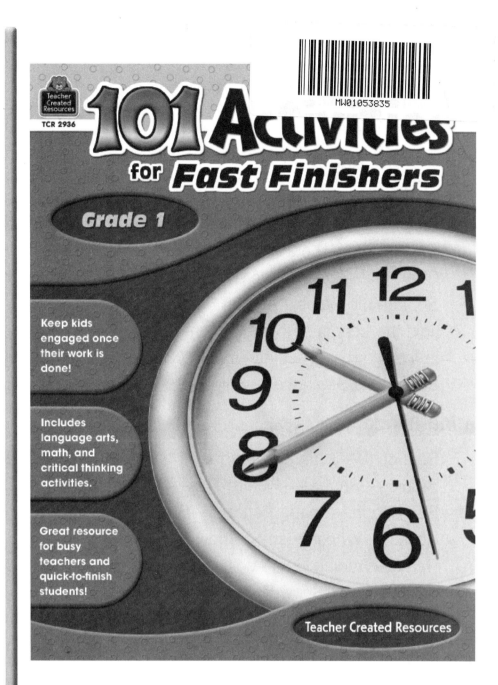

TCR 2936

101 Activities for *Fast Finishers*

Grade 1

- Keep kids engaged once their work is done!
- Includes language arts, math, and critical thinking activities.
- Great resource for busy teachers and quick-to-finish students!

Teacher Created Resources

Teacher Created Resources
6421 Industry Way
Westminster, CA 92683
www.teachercreated.com

ISBN: 978-1-4206-2936-1

© *2011 Teacher Created Resources*
Made in U.S.A.

Teacher Created Resources

TABLE OF CONTENTS

Making Words—Add Ons 1— Add Ons 2—Fitting Words—Name It—
Picture Crosswords—Letter Add—Make It Up—Writing Vowel Sounds—
Small Words—Letter Pairs—Scrambled Up—Drop a Letter—First Letters—
Change the Order—Word Color—Sentence Make—Change the Sound—
Sounds the Same—Animal Find—Alphabetical Order—Changing Letters—
Join the Letters—Rhyme Time—Rhymes—Change It—Vowel Sort—Where
in the Word?—Check It—Writing Sentences—Which Word?—Which One?—
Scrambled Sentences—Silly Story—Cat Fight

Sets of 10—Square Search—Ordering—Adding On—Position—Shape
Riddles—Shapes—Picture This—Right and Wrong—Odds and Evens—
Fishy Facts—Shape Patterns—Shaping Up—What Comes Next?—What
Socks?—Whose Fish?—Show Addition—Circles—Equal Sums—Get
Ready—Adding Up—Addition Crossword—Missing Addends—Connect
the Answers—Show Subtraction—Show the Picture—Subtraction Riddle—
Color Code—What's the Sign?—Say It In Code—Math Path—Comparing
Numbers—Find the Numbers—Number Clues—Number Riddles

Find the Pair—Alphabet Maze—Copy Cats—What Comes Next?—Out of
Place—Sock Match—Half a Picture—Careful Color—Scrambled Colors—
Add On—Inside and Outside—Tricky Shapes—Connect the Dots—The
Same—Bob's Kite—Hidden Pictures—Map Madness—Color In—Match
Up—Crossword Puzzler—Time to Draw—Change It Up—Color Ins—Read
and Draw—Whose Ball?—Math Triangles—Hidden Animals—Pay For It—
Visiting Friends—What's the Same?—Who Ate What?

INTRODUCTION

All students work at different speeds. Many take about the same amount of time to finish their work. Some are slower than others, and some are faster than others. You've probably been asked, "I'm done, what do I do now?" more times than you can count. But what's a teacher to do when one or more students finish early? The activity pages in *101 Activities for Fast Finishers* are the answer.

The 101 activities in this book focus on language arts, math, and critical thinking, and are divided as follows:

- Lively Language Arts (35 activities)
- Mind-Bender Math (35 activities)
- Beyond Brainy (31 activities)

Each activity has been labeled with an approximate amount of time that it will take students to complete. The estimated times range from 5 to 15 minutes. It is recommended that you copy, in advance, several pages representing the different times, and have them on hand to distribute, as needed. When a student asks you that famous "What do I do now?" question, a quick look at the clock will tell you which activity to give him or her. These activities will also be helpful to keep in your emergency substitute file as filler activities.

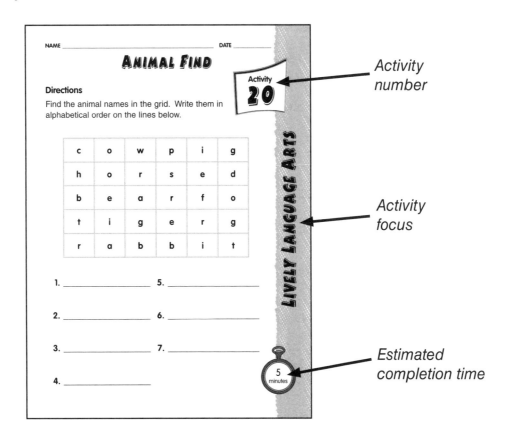

MAKING WORDS

Directions

Make words to match the pictures.
Use one letter from each box.

p	u	n
s	i	t
p	e	g
d	o	n
h	a	g

1. _____ _____ _____

2. _____ _____ _____

3. _____ _____ _____

4. _____ _____ _____

5. _____ _____ _____

5
minutes

LIVELY LANGUAGE ARTS

ADD ONS 1

Directions

Add "ow" in the spaces, and then draw lines to the pictures that match the words. Write a sentence using one of the words on the line below.

1. c l ___ ___ n

2. c r ___ ___ n

3. s n ___ ___

4. b ___ ___ l

5. t ___ ___ n

5 minutes

_____

ADD ONS 2

Activity 3

Directions

Add "ai" in the spaces, and then draw a line to each picture that matches a word. Write a sentence using word number 2 below.

1. s _____ _____ l

2. r _____ _____ n

3. tr _____ _____ n

4. ch _____ _____ n

5. m _____ _____ l

6. t _____ _____ l

7. sn _____ _____ l

8. br _____ _____ n

_____

5 minutes

FITTING WORDS

Activity
4

Directions

Read the words in each group. Write the word that has the right shape to fit inside the boxes. The first one has been done for you.

1. mad
pad
dad

3. jam
him
ram

5. fun
pin
can

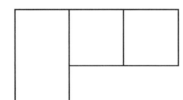

2. top
gap
cup

4. beg
sag
rug

6. let
cat
got

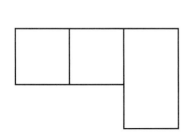

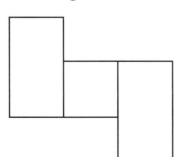

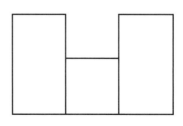

LIVELY LANGUAGE ARTS

5
minutes

NAME IT

Directions

Make words to name the pictures using the letters in the box. You may use a letter more than once.

n	f	x	p	b
	t	m	a	o	

1.  _____

4.  _____

2. _____ _____

5. _____

3.  _____

6.  _____

5 minutes

LIVELY LANGUAGE ARTS

PICTURE CROSSWORDS

Activity

6

Directions

Write the words that match the pictures in the crossword squares. The arrows will show you where to start each word.

1.

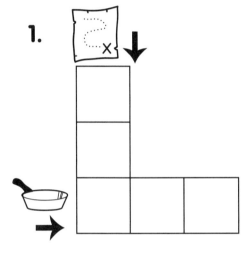

3.

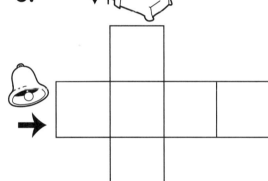

2.

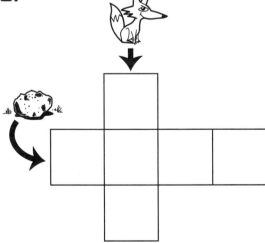

4.

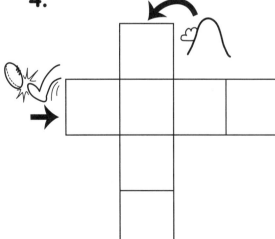

5 minutes

LETTER ADD

Directions

Add a letter to make a word that matches each picture.

1.  ____old

2. ____tar

3. ____ing

4. ____rum

5. ____hip

6.  ____lag

7.  ____heel

8.  ____room

LIVELY LANGUAGE ARTS

5 minutes

MAKE IT UP

Activity

8

Directions

Use the letters in the box to make the words that match the pictures below. Cross out each letter as you use it.

x	b	f
c	o	b
u	a	d
p	t	e

1. _____

2. _____

3. _____

4. _____

5 minutes

LIVELY LANGUAGE ARTS

WRITING VOWEL SOUNDS

Activity
9

Directions

Say the name of the picture, and then say the vowel sound. Write the short vowel sound on the line.

1.  k____ck

5. w____b

2.  v____n

6.  sw____m

3.  l____g

7. c____p

4.  w____g

8.  w____ll

5
minutes

12

LIVELY LANGUAGE ARTS

SMALL WORDS

Activity
10

Directions

Look at the small words in the box. Add the correct small word to the letters below to make the word that matches each picture.

eat	lag	tar	art
now	oat	old	our

1. s

5. g_____

2. m

6. c_____

3. f_____

7. f_____

4. c

8. s_____

5
minutes

LIVELY LANGUAGE ARTS

LETTER PAIRS

LIVELY LANGUAGE ARTS

Directions

Add "ee" or "oo" in the spaces below to make the words that match the pictures.

1.

m ___ ___ n

4.

br ___ ___ m

7.

sl ___ ___ p

2.

qu ___ ___ n

5.

t ___ ___ th

8.

d ___ ___ r

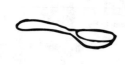

3.

sp ___ ___ n

6.

f ___ ___ t

9.

s ___ ___ ds

5 minutes

Another "ee" word is [   ] .

Scrambled Up

Activity
12

Directions

Unscramble the letters to find the words that match the pictures. Write them on the lines.

1. | a b l l |

_____

2. | n t s e |

_____

3. | p i s h |

_____

4. | r t s a |

_____

5. | l c k o |

_____

6. | m u d r |

_____

LIVELY LANGUAGE ARTS

5 minutes

DROP A LETTER

Directions

In each word, cross out a letter to make a new word that matches the picture. Write the new word on the line.

LIVELY LANGUAGE ARTS

1. meat

_____

4. carve

_____

2. train

_____

5. broom

_____

3. wheel

_____

6. bring

_____

5
minutes

FIRST LETTERS

Directions

Choose the correct letter pair in the box to make the word that matches the picture. Write it on the line.

Activity
14

1. | sh   sl |

_____ip

4. | sh   sn |

_____ow

7. | sw   sk |

_____im

2. | sn   st |

_____ake

5. | fr   fl |

_____ower

8. | bl   br |

_____ick

3. | sh   st |

_____oe

6. | tr   th |

_____uck

9. | sn   st |

_____ail

5
minutes

LIVELY LANGUAGE ARTS

CHANGE THE ORDER

Activity
15

Directions

Change the order of the letters to make the word match the picture.

LIVELY LANGUAGE ARTS

1.  tar _____

2. ram _____

3. nap _____

4.  was _____

5. **10** net _____

6. tan _____

5 minutes

WORD COLOR

Directions

Look at the words in the grid. Color the spaces with names of **toys red**, **animals blue**, and **birds yellow**. One of the words is a toy and an animal. Color that space **green**.

eagle	zebra	top
bat	ball	horse
tiger	hawk	doll
swan	crow	duck
pig	kite	mouse

5 minutes

LIVELY LANGUAGE ARTS

SENTENCE MAKE

LIVELY LANGUAGE ARTS

Directions

Write the first letter of the name of each picture to make some words. (The first one is done for you.) All the words together make a sentence. What is it? Write the sentence on the line at the bottom.

A _____

_____   _____   _____

_____   _____   _____

_____   _____   _____

_____   _____

5 minutes

_____

CHANGE THE SOUND

Directions

Change the letters that make the beginning sound to form new words. Write the new words on the lines.

1. change	fan	to		_____
2. change	cat	to		_____
3. change	pen	to		_____
4. change	jet	to		_____
5. change	wig	to		_____
6. change	fin	to		_____
7. change	top	to		_____
8. change	hug	to		_____

LIVELY LANGUAGE ARTS

10
minutes

SOUNDS THE SAME

Directions

Each pair of words below sounds the same, but means something different. Draw the missing picture to show its meaning.

1.

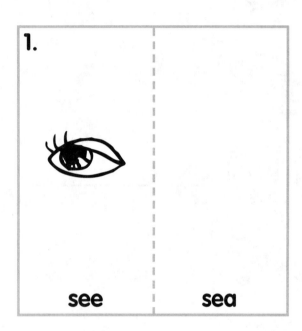

| see | sea |

3.

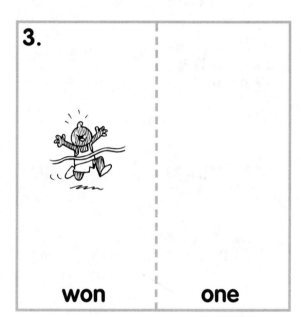

| won | one |

2.

| son | sun |

4.

| bawl | ball |

5 minutes

LIVELY LANGUAGE ARTS

ANIMAL FIND

Activity
20

Directions

Find the animal names in the grid. Write them in alphabetical order on the lines below.

c	o	w	p	i	g
h	o	r	s	e	d
b	e	a	r	f	o
t	i	g	e	r	g
r	a	b	b	i	t

LIVELY LANGUAGE ARTS

1. _____   5. _____

2. _____   6. _____

3. _____   7. _____

4. _____

5
minutes

ALPHABETICAL ORDER

Activity
21

Directions

Write the words in alphabetical order on the lines below.

mirror	baby
football	monkey
bath	dress
igloo	wombat
wooly	ice
dash	foot

1. _____

2. _____

3. _____

4. _____

5. _____

6. _____

7. _____

8. _____

9. _____

10. _____

11. _____

12. _____

LIVELY LANGUAGE ARTS

10 minutes

CHANGING LETTERS

Directions

Change the **first** letter in each word to make a new word that matches the picture.

1.

cool

_____

2.

bake

_____

3.

silk

_____

4.

hard

_____

5.

coat

_____

6.

sing

_____

7.

bear

_____

8.

pain

_____

9.

luck

_____

5
minutes

JOIN THE LETTERS

Activity
23

Directions

Join the letter in each box to the letter pairs to make eight words. Write the words, and then draw pictures of four of them in the box below.

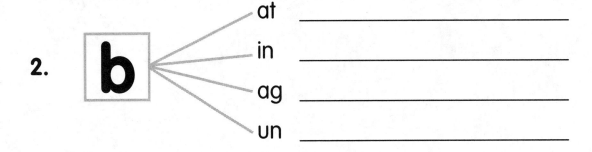

1. **C**

at _____

an _____

ap _____

ar _____

2. **b**

at _____

in _____

ag _____

un _____

10 minutes

RHYME TIME

Activity 24

Directions

Which rhyming word is correct? Write it on the line to complete each sentence.

1. | sun / run

The _____ is shining in the sky.

2. | bat / cat

I saw our _____ catch a mouse.

3. | peg / leg

Tom fell and hurt his _____ .

4. | big / fig

An elephant is a _____ animal.

5. | dry / fry

Dad will _____ the fish in the hot oil.

5 minutes

RHYMES

Activity
25

Directions

Write four words that rhyme with each word below.

pen

_____

_____

_____

_____

bee

_____

_____

_____

_____

to

_____

_____

_____

_____

pop

_____

_____

_____

_____

hat

_____

_____

_____

_____

keep

_____

_____

_____

_____

10
minutes

Change It

Directions

Change the beginning sound of the underlined word to make a new word that completes each sentence. Use the correct word from the box.

1. The <u>cat</u> wore a _____.

2. The _____ went for a <u>jog</u>.

3. We had <u>fun</u> in the _____.

4. What did you _____ in the <u>net</u>?

5. The <u>dad</u> was very _____.

6. A _____ had a <u>fan</u>.

7. The <u>pig</u> began to _____.

8. There were _____ <u>men</u>.

sun

get

sad

dig

dog

man

ten

hat

10
minutes

LIVELY LANGUAGE ARTS

VOWEL SORT

Activity 27

Directions

Read the words below. Listen for the **long** or **short** vowel sound. Write the words in the correct column.

mule	yet	plug	juice	cut
cab	stub	fed	boat	leap
best	dock	plan	fog	take
stick	bride	grape	line	snap
blame	spot	green	rip	eel
like	woke	swim	note	cute

Short A	Short E	Short I	Short O	Short U
Long A	**Long E**	**Long I**	**Long O**	**Long U**

10 minutes

LIVELY LANGUAGE ARTS

WHERE IN THE WORD?

Activity
28

Directions

Use every word in the box to complete the chart below. Find the words that have the beginning, middle, and final consonant of that specific letter. Write the words in the correct column.

gift	play	milk	leaf	vest
runt	rain	lid	fall	camel
bus	cup	sack	apple	
duck	gum	nut	ladder	

	Beginning Consonant	Middle Consonant	Final Consonant
d			
f			
m			
n			
p			
s			

LIVELY LANGUAGE ARTS

10
minutes

CHECK IT

Activity
29

Directions

Look at the picture, and then read the sentences underneath it. Which sentence matches the picture? Put a check next to the correct sentence.

1.

He cut up the fog. ☐

He cut up the log. ☐

2.

Hop on the mess. ☐

Mop up the mess. ☐

3.

She runs in the mud. ☐

She sits in the mud. ☐

4.

A bat sits on Mom. ☐

A cat sits on Mom. ☐

5
minutes

LIVELY LANGUAGE ARTS

WRITING SENTENCES

Activity 30

Directions

Choose one word or phrase from each column below to help you write **complete sentences.** Use each word or phrase only once.

Who	Did What	Where
My teacher	sang	on our street.
I	laughed	at school.
Sally	ate	in the rain.
The dog	ran	by the tree.

1. _____

2. _____

3. _____

4. _____

10 minutes

LIVELY LANGUAGE ARTS

WHICH WORD?

Activity 31

Directions

Choose the correct word in **bold** to complete each sentence. Circle it.

1. Tom went to the store to buy some (**bumps milk holes**).

2. When we go camping, we sleep in a (**box string tent**).

3. When babies are hungry they often (**cry swim rich**).

4. If you go to the zoo, you may see a (**letter monkey smell**).

5. A (**spring ticket rabbit**) is an animal with long ears and soft fur.

6. The lion (**book ran crawled**) after the animals in the jungle.

WHICH ONE?

Activity
32

Directions

Circle the correct answer to each question. Then draw pictures of the answers in the space below.

1. Which one is an insect?   **cup   bee   dog**

2. Which one is a fruit?   **pea   tiger   banana**

3. Which one is a flower?   **rose   book   can**

4. Which one is an animal?   **pencil   zebra   tree**

5. Which one is a vegetable?   **carrot   bottle   paper**

LIVELY LANGUAGE ARTS

5 minutes

SCRAMBLED SENTENCES

Activity
33

Directions

Put the words below in order to make a sentence.

1. dog so The is cute.

_____

2. just She puppies had eight.

_____

3. were two There black puppies.

_____

4. Five were puppies brown.

_____

5. last the What was of color the one?

_____

10
minutes

SILLY STORY

Activity
34

Directions

Write a strange story to share with your friends.
Fill in the blanks in the box, but do not look ahead
at the story. Then use the words to complete your
strange tale and read your story out loud.

1. month of year _____	**6.** food _____
2. an illness _____	**7.** action word _____
3. name of a place _____	**8.** action word _____
4. name of a person _____	**9.** name of a thing_____
5. food _____	**10.** food _____

One cloudy, stormy day in _____ , Frankie

1

woke up with a _____ . His mother made him stay

2

in _____ all day. He fell asleep dreaming about

3

pirates. Suddenly, a loud pirate named _____

4

shook him and told him to eat sloppy _____

5

and hard _____ for breakfast. Another angry

6

pirate made him _____ over large pillows and

7

_____ beanbags across his bedroom. A

8

third pirate grabbed him out of bed and made him get on the

great big _____ and sail the high seas. The

9

waves were crashing. All of a sudden, Frankie's mom shook

him awake. She scared off the mean pirates and fed him

_____ for lunch! He was safe from danger now!

10

15
minutes

LIVELY LANGUAGE ARTS

NAME _____   DATE _____

CAT FIGHT

Activity
35

Directions

Write a strange story to share with your friends. Fill in the blanks in the box, but do not look ahead at the story. Then use the words to complete your strange tale and read your story out loud.

LIVELY LANGUAGE ARTS

1. kitchen tool _____
2. loud noise _____
3. day of the week _____
4. boy's name _____
5. boy's name _____
6. shape (more than one) _____

7. cat body part _____
8. a last name _____
9. food (more than one) _____
10. animal sound _____
11. food (from #9) _____

Grab the _____ ! Crash! Bang! Boom!
_____ ! On _____
afternoon, noises were coming from everywhere! Two large
cats were fighting on the street corner. The biggest cat,
_____ , was mad at the smaller cat,
_____ . Both cats wanted to play in the
empty lot at the corner. They spit at each other. They ran in
_____ . A _____ was flying in
all directions! Suddenly, up came the big cat's owner,
Mr. _____ . Both cats saw the two
_____ in his hands. He grinned at them.
Enough fighting, boys! They _____ sweetly.
The _____ looked better than the fight!

15 minutes

SETS OF 10

Activity
36

Directions

Color a set of ten in each group.

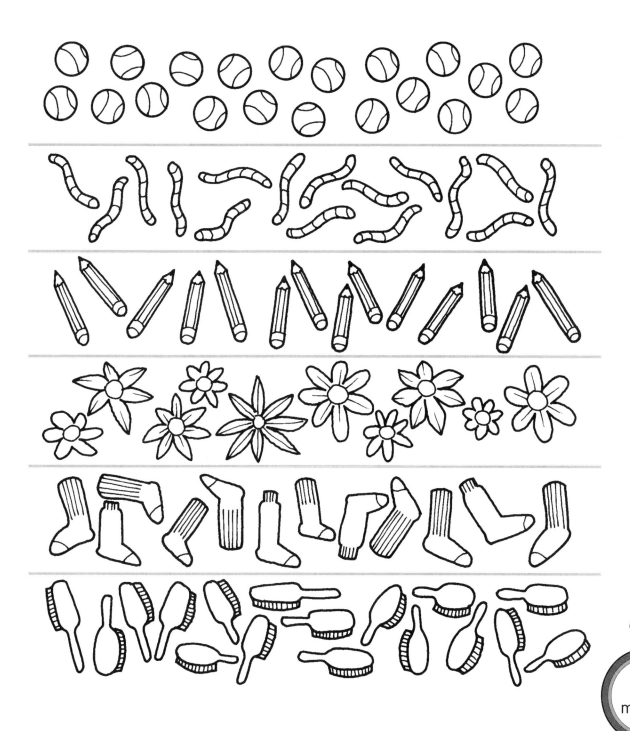

MIND-BENDER MATH

10
minutes

SQUARE SEARCH

Activity 37

Directions

Look closely at the picture.
Count all the squares.

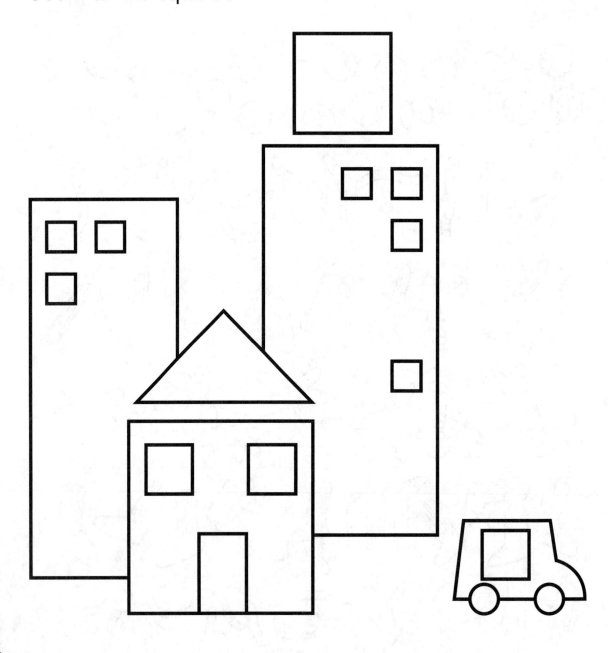

5 minutes

There are _____ squares.

ORDERING

Activity
38

Directions

Color the row of balls following the instructions below.

1st

1. Color the third ball yellow.

2. Color the fifth ball pink.

3. Color the second ball brown.

4. Color the fourth ball green.

5. Color the sixth ball red.

6. Color the first ball orange.

5 minutes

ADDING ON

Directions

In each row, draw the extra pictures to make up the number shown.

5	
8	
6	
7	
4	

MIND-BENDER MATH

10 minutes

NAME ______________________ DATE __________

POSITION

Activity
40

Directions

Circle the picture that is in the position shown at the beginning of each row.

1st	
5th	
8th	
6th	
3rd	
4th	
9th	
7th	
2nd	
10th	

MIND-BENDER MATH

5 minutes

SHAPE RIDDLES

Activity **41**

Directions

Read the clues below to solve each riddle. Use the shapes to help you. Write your answers below the clues.

triangle

circle

square

rectangle

hexagon

pentagon

1. I have 3 sides and 3 corners.	**4.** I have 5 sides and 5 corners.
2. I have 6 sides and 6 corners.	**5.** I have 2 long sides, 2 short sides, and 4 corners.
3. I do not have any corners.	**6.** I have 4 corners and 4 equal sides.

10 minutes

SHAPES

Activity
42

Directions

Color all squares blue.

Color all triangles yellow.

Color all rectangles green.

Color all circles red.

5
minutes

PICTURE THIS

Directions

There are a number of different types of things shown in this picture. How many of each different thing can you see? Count them and write the numbers in the boxes.

 birds ☐

 cat ☐

 flowers ☐

 sheep ☐

 dogs ☐

 people ☐

 pigs ☐

 trees ☐

 ducks ☐

10 minutes

MIND-BENDER MATH

RIGHT AND WRONG

Activity
44

Directions

Color **green** the leaves with a **right** answer.
Color **brown** those that have a **wrong** answer.

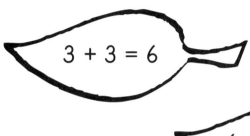

$3 + 3 = 6$

$7 + 5 = 12$

$6 + 4 = 10$

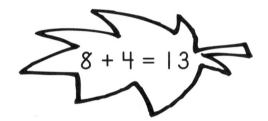

$8 + 4 = 13$

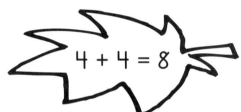

$4 + 4 = 8$

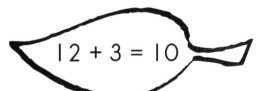

$12 + 3 = 10$

$8 + 8 = 12$

$6 + 7 = 13$

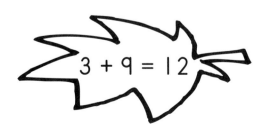

$3 + 9 = 12$

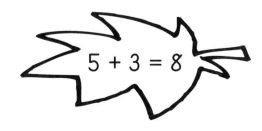

$5 + 3 = 8$

5 minutes

MIND-BENDER MATH

ODDS AND EVENS

Directions

Color **blue** all the balloons that have an **odd** number for an answer. Color **red** all the balloons with an **even** number.

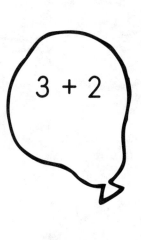

3 + 2

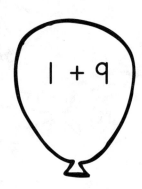

1 + 9

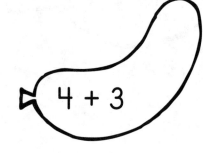

4 + 3

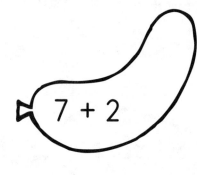

7 + 2

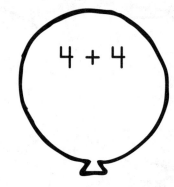

4 + 4

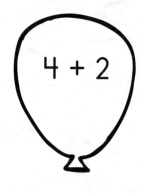

4 + 2

6 + 3

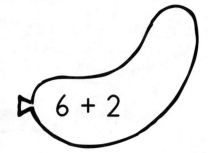

6 + 2

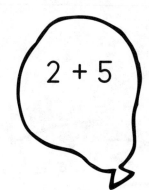

2 + 5

MIND-BENDER MATH

5 minutes

FISHY FACTS

Directions

All the fish Tommy caught have the correct answer on them. Color the fish that Tommy caught.

$8 + 3 = 12$

$6 + 4 = 10$

$9 + 3 = 12$

$8 + 5 = 12$

$10 - 4 = 6$

$12 - 7 = 4$

$12 - 3 = 9$

$8 - 5 = 3$

$14 - 4 = 10$

MIND-BENDER MATH

5 minutes

SHAPE PATTERNS

Activity
47

Directions

Draw the shape that comes next in each pattern.

1. ○ ○ □ □ △ △ ○ ○ □ □ _____

2. △ □ ⬠ ○ △ □ ⬠ ○ _____

3. △ ▽ △ ▽ △ ▽ △ ▽ △ ▽ _____

4. ⋀ ○ △ □ ⋀ ○ △ □ _____

5. ⬭ △ ○ ⊰ □ ⬭ △ ○ _____

5
minutes

MIND-BENDER MATH

SHAPING UP

Activity
48

Directions

Color triangles △ red. Color squares ☐ blue.
Color rectangles ▭ yellow. Color circles ◯ green.
Count the shapes. Write how many below.

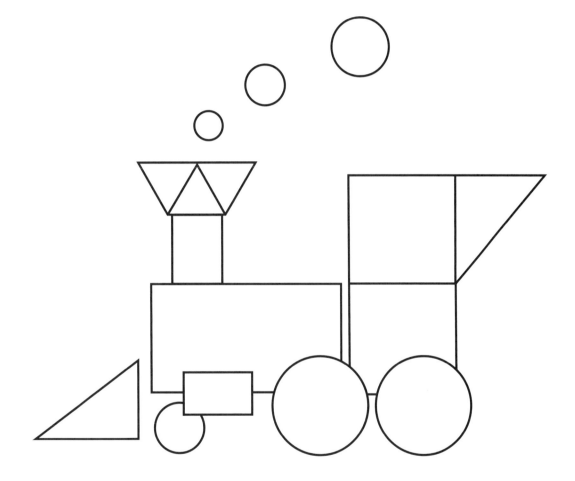

How many?

△ = _____   ☐ = _____

▭ = _____   ◯ = _____

5
minutes

WHAT COMES NEXT?

Activity 49

Directions

Write the next two numbers in each pattern.

MIND-BENDER MATH

1. 1, 2, 3, 4, 5, 6, 7, 8, _____ , _____

2. 2, 4, 6, 8, 10, 12, 14, 16, _____ , _____

3. 1, 3, 5, 7, 9, 11, 13, 15, _____ , _____

4. 1, 1, 2, 2, 3, 3, 4, 4, _____ , _____

5. 9, 8, 7, 6, 5, 4, 3, 2, _____ , _____

6. 5, 10, 15, 20, 25, 30, 35, 40, _____ , _____

7. 1, 4, 7, 10, 13, 16, 19, 22, _____ , _____

8. 10, 20, 30, 40, 50, 60, 70, 80, _____ , _____

9. 18, 16, 14, 12, 10, 8, 6, 4, _____ , _____

10. 0, 1, 0, 2, 0, 3, 0, 4, _____ , _____

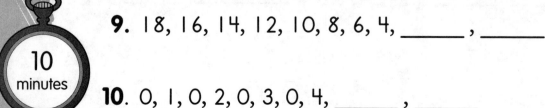

10 minutes

WHAT SOCKS?

Activity 50

Directions

Can you find the matching socks? They are socks that have exactly the same answers. Color each pair of socks a different color.

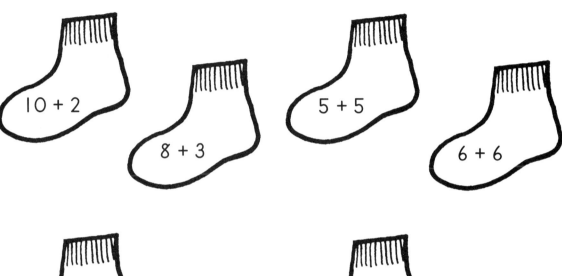

10 + 2

8 + 3

5 + 5

6 + 6

2 + 5

8 + 5

6 + 7

6 + 4

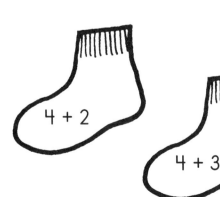

4 + 2

4 + 3

1 + 5

6 + 5

10 minutes

MIND-BENDER MATH

WHOSE FISH?

Activity
51

Directions

James catches only fish that have an **odd** number for their answer. Color them **red**. Jackie catches only fish that have an **even** number for their answer. Color them **blue**.

MIND-BENDER MATH

3 + 5

8 + 5

10 – 4

12 – 6

5 + 4

12 – 3

7 – 2

7 + 2

9 + 3

11 – 3

10 minutes

SHOW ADDITION

Activity
52

Directions

Write a number sentence to go with each picture.

MIND-BENDER MATH

1.

_____ + _____ = _____

4.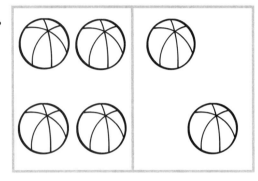

_____ + _____ = _____

2.

_____ + _____ = _____

5.

_____ + _____ = _____

3.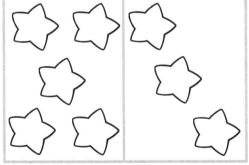

_____ + _____ = _____

6.

_____ + _____ = _____

5 minutes

CIRCLES

Directions

Color the two numbers that add up to the number in the center of each circle. The first one has been done for you.

1.
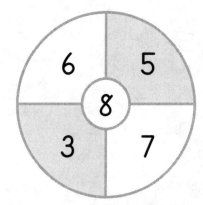

4.
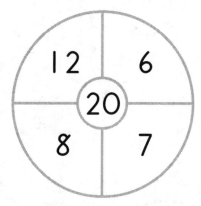

2.
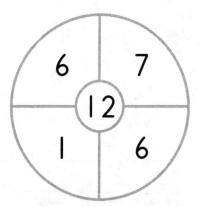

5.
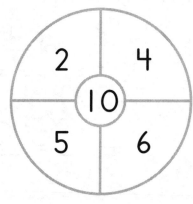

3.
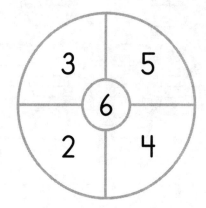

6.
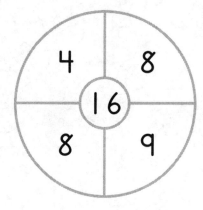

10 minutes

NAME _____   DATE _____

EQUAL SUMS

Directions

Circle the addends that equal the sum in each cloud. There is more than one way to equal each sum.

1.
| 2 + 2 | 5 + 4 | 3 + 5 | 7 + 1 | 6 + 2 | 4 + 3 |

2.
| 2 + 2 | 3 + 2 | 4 + 0 | 5 + 1 | 3 + 1 | 0 + 4 |

3.
| 6 + 0 | 2 + 5 | 4 + 2 | 3 + 3 | 5 + 1 | 6 + 2 |

4.
| 2 + 0 | 3 + 1 | 4 + 1 | 1 + 1 | 0 + 2 | 1 + 2 |

5.
| 4 + 6 | 3 + 6 | 1 + 8 | 1 + 9 | 8 + 2 | 9 + 0 |

6.
| 3 + 1 | 2 + 0 | 3 + 0 | 2 + 1 | 0 + 3 | 1 + 2 |

7.
| 6 + 1 | 2 + 5 | 3 + 5 | 6 + 3 | 4 + 3 | 7 + 0 |

8.
| 2 + 2 | 5 + 0 | 3 + 2 | 1 + 4 | 4 + 2 | 2 + 3 |

MIND-BENDER MATH

GET READY

Activity
55

Directions

The cars are ready to begin the race.
But before they can start, you must find
the number to put in the back wheel so that both wheels
add up to the number on the car.

MIND-BENDER MATH

1.

4.

2.

5.

3.

6.

10 minutes

ADDING UP

Activity
56

Directions

Cross out each answer in the balloons as you solve the problems.

1.
$0 + 6 =$

5.
$1 + 10 =$

9.
$2 + 3 =$

2.
$3 + 5 =$

6.
$4 + 7 =$

10.
$5 + 9 =$

3.
$6 + 8 =$

7.
$7 + 4 =$

11.
$8 + 2 =$

4.
$9 + 5 =$

8.
$10 + 9 =$

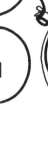

19 5 11 10 14 14
14 11 8 11 6

10 minutes

ADDITION CROSSWORD

Activity
57

Directions

Solve each addition problem. Write the number names in the crossword puzzle.

MIND-BENDER MATH

Across

1. 8 + 6 =

2. 10 + 7 =

3. 7 + 5 =

4. 9 + 9 =

Down

3. 14 + 6 =

5. 6 + 7 =

6. 9 + 6 =

7. 8 + 2 =

8. 5 + 6 =

9. 12 + 7 =

10. 8 + 8 =

Word Bank

ten

eleven

twelve

thirteen

fourteen

fifteen

sixteen

seventeen

eighteen

nineteen

twenty

10
minutes

MISSING ADDENDS

Activity **58**

Directions

Find the missing addends. Then match each addend to the numbers in the box below. Write the matching letter in each blank to solve the riddle.

Why did the chicken cross the playground?

1. $3 + \boxed{} = 4$

   E

2. $3 + \boxed{} = 8$

   H

3. $\boxed{} + 5 = 9$

   R

4. $4 + \boxed{} = 7$

   O

5. $\boxed{} + 5 = 7$

   T

6. $\boxed{} + 0 = 10$

   D

7. $\boxed{} + 2 = 9$

   I

8. $8 + \boxed{} = 8$

   S

9. $1 + \boxed{} = 9$

   L

10. $3 + \boxed{} = 9$

    G

$$\overline{\ }\ \overline{\ }\quad \overline{\ }\ \overline{\ }\ \overline{\ }\quad \overline{\ }\ \overline{\ }\quad \overline{\ }\ \overline{\ }\ \overline{\ }$$
$$2\ 3\qquad 6\ 1\ 2\qquad 2\ 3\qquad 2\ 5\ 1$$

$$\overline{\ }\ \overline{\ }\ \overline{\ }\ \overline{\ }\ \overline{\ }\qquad\qquad \overline{\ }\ \overline{\ }\ \overline{\ }\ \overline{\ }\ \overline{\ }$$
$$3\ 2\ 5\ 1\ 4\qquad\qquad 0\ 8\ 7\ 10\ 1$$

MIND-BENDER MATH

10 minutes

CONNECT THE ANSWERS

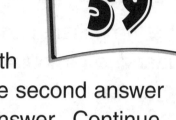

Activity
59

Directions

To discover the secret shape, find the sums and then connect the answers with a line. Connect the first answer with the second answer and the second answer with the third answer. Continue until you finish the shape.

1.

```
   17
+ 22
```

3.

```
   76
+ 22
```

5.

```
   70
+ 20
```

7.

```
   51
+ 27
```

9.

```
   62
+ 22
```

2.

```
   54
+ 21
```

4.

```
   18
+ 31
```

6.

```
   11
+ 11
```

8.

```
   19
+ 10
```

10.

```
   35
+ 21
```

39 •

98 •

75 •

56 •

84 •

49 •

• 29

22 •

90 •

• 78

10
minutes

62

SHOW SUBTRACTION

Activity
60

Directions

Write a number sentence to go with each picture.

1.

_____ – _____ = _____

4.
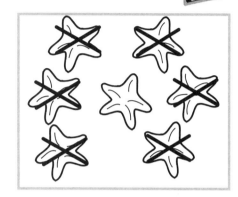

_____ – _____ = _____

2.
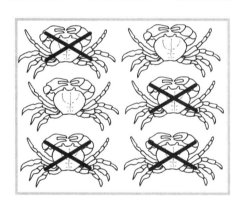

_____ – _____ = _____

5.
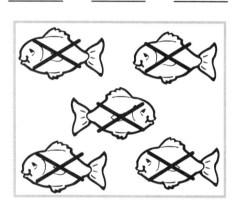

_____ – _____ = _____

3.

_____ – _____ = _____

6.

_____ – _____ = _____

MIND-BENDER MATH

5 minutes

SHOW THE PICTURE

Activity

61

Directions

Match the number sentence on the left with the correct picture on the right.

1. 5 – 3 = 2

A.

2. 4 – 1 = 3

B.

3. 2 – 2 = 0

C.

4. 3 – 0 = 3

D.

5. 4 – 2 = 2

E.

6. 7 – 2 = 5

F.

5 minutes

MIND-BENDER MATH

SUBTRACTION RIDDLE

Activity
62

Directions

Solve each problem. Then match each answer to the numbers in the box below. Write the matching letter in each blank to solve the riddle.

Why are seagulls called seagulls?

1. $\begin{array}{r} 9 \\ -4 \\ \hline \end{array}$ (R)

4. $\begin{array}{r} 14 \\ -5 \\ \hline \end{array}$ (G)

7. $\begin{array}{r} 19 \\ -7 \\ \hline \end{array}$ (Y)

10. $\begin{array}{r} 12 \\ -5 \\ \hline \end{array}$ (T)

2. $\begin{array}{r} 14 \\ -3 \\ \hline \end{array}$ (A)

5. $\begin{array}{r} 16 \\ -6 \\ \hline \end{array}$ (S)

8. $\begin{array}{r} 19 \\ -6 \\ \hline \end{array}$ (L)

11. $\begin{array}{r} 17 \\ -8 \\ \hline \end{array}$ (G)

3. $\begin{array}{r} 15 \\ -7 \\ \hline \end{array}$ (B)

6. $\begin{array}{r} 14 \\ -5 \\ \hline \end{array}$ (G)

9. $\begin{array}{r} 13 \\ -7 \\ \hline \end{array}$ (E)

12. $\begin{array}{r} 18 \\ -6 \\ \hline \end{array}$ (Y)

If they lived by the _____ _____ _____ , they would be
               8   11   12

called _____ _____ _____ _____ _____ _____ .
       8   11   9   6   13   10

10 minutes

MIND-BENDER MATH

COLOR CODE

Activity
63

Directions

Solve the number sentences in the rectangles. Then use the color code below to color the rectangles in the correct color.

3 = blue	5 = orange	7 = pink
4 = red	6 = yellow	8 = green

MIND-BENDER MATH

1. 16 − 10 =	6. 12 − 6 =	11. 10 − 5 =	16. 2 + 2 =
2. 4 + 4 =	**7.** 10 − 7 =	**12.** 10 − 3 =	**17.** 7 − 4 =
3. 10 − 4 =	**8.** 12 − 8 =	**13.** 6 − 3 =	**18.** 4 + 3 =
4. 8 − 2 =	**9.** 12 − 7 =	**14.** 10 − 6 =	**19.** 6 + 2 =
5. 20 − 15 =	**10.** 10 − 2 =	**15.** 14 − 10 =	**20.** 12 − 4 =

10 minutes

WHAT'S THE SIGN?

Activity **64**

Directions

Fill in the missing **+**, **−**, or **=** sign in each box.

1. 3 ☐ 2 = 5

7. 9 ☐ 6 = 3

2. 6 − 1 ☐ 5

8. 6 + 2 ☐ 8

3. 9 ☐ 3 = 6

9. 10 ☐ 5 = 15

4. 2 ☐ 7 = 9

10. 12 ☐ 6 = 6

5. 1 ☐ 3 = 4

11. 14 ☐ 4 = 10

6. 4 + 3 ☐ 7

12. 7 ☐ 5 = 12

MIND-BENDER MATH

10
minutes

SAY IT IN CODE

Activity
65

Directions

Solve each math problem. Write the letter that goes with each answer in the box.
Use the code to discover the answer.

1. What did the camera say to the mouse?

A	C	E	H	S	Y
3	1	5	2	0	4

$$\begin{array}{cccccccc} 0 & 2 & 1 & & 1 & 1 & 3 & 4 & 0 & 5 \\ +0 & +1 & +3 & & +0 & +1 & +2 & +1 & +0 & +0 \end{array}$$

☐ ☐ ☐   ☐ ☐ ☐ ☐ ☐ ☐ !

---

2. What did the pebble say to the rock?

E	L	O	R	S	T
1	4	3	0	5	2

$$\begin{array}{cccccccc} 6 & 2 & 5 & 5 & & 4 & 6 & 5 & 4 \\ -2 & -1 & -3 & -0 & & -4 & -3 & -1 & -0 \end{array}$$

☐ ☐ ☐ ☐ '   ☐ ☐ ☐ ☐ !

10
minutes

MATH PATH

Activity
66

Directions

Fill in the blank boxes as you follow the path. If the operation says add, add the two numbers together. If it says subtract, take away the second number and fill in the answer box. The first answer box has been done for you.

Start ⟹ $5 - 2 = 3 + 1 =$ [ ]

$4 + \;[\;] = 3 - [\;] = 2 +$ [ ]

$= \;[\;] - 1 = [\;] - 2 = [\;] +$ [1]

$[\;] = 1 + [\;] = 4 + [\;] =$

$2 = [\;] - 3 = [\;]$ **Finish!**

10 minutes

COMPARING NUMBERS

Activity
67

Directions

Compare the numbers using >, <, and =.
The first one has been done for you.

MIND-BENDER MATH

1. 43 (<) 62	**6.** 73 ◯ 31	**11.** 57 ◯ 76
2. 67 ◯ 47	**7.** 39 ◯ 44	**12.** 58 ◯ 43
3. 39 ◯ 26	**8.** 73 ◯ 73	**13.** 42 ◯ 52
4. 28 ◯ 19	**9.** 83 ◯ 74	**14.** 18 ◯ 38
5. 19 ◯ 19	**10.** 93 ◯ 97	**15.** 48 ◯ 36

10 minutes

FIND THE NUMBERS

Activity
68

Directions

Use the clues to circle the correct number or numbers.

1. Circle the numbers that have a 4 in the tens place.

43   29   63   41   78   37   49

2. Circle the numbers that have a 9 in the ones place.

19   97   58   79   63   9   29

3. Circle the number that has 2 tens and 5 ones.

35   57   52   26   25   53   16

4. Circle the numbers that have no ones.

21   60   43   30   76   43   75

5. Circle the numbers that have no tens.

43   7   17   8   2   59   36

6. Circle the number that has a 1 in the hundreds place.

10   61   100   43   90   82   41

7. Circle the numbers that you say when you count by 10s.

40   62   90   85   100   34   67

8. Circle the numbers that you say when you count by 5s.

5   27   30   43   50   65   72

10 minutes

NUMBER CLUES

Activity
69

Directions

Read the clues to determine the correct number. Write it on the line.

1. I am thinking of a number.

It is greater than 21.

It is less than 23.

What is the number? _____

2. I am thinking of a number.

It is less than 40.

It is greater than 30.

You say it when you count by 5s.

What is the number? _____

3. I am thinking of a number.

It has a 2 in the ones place.

It has a 7 in the tens place.

What is the number? _____

4. I am thinking of a number.

It is less than 20.

It has a 0 in the ones place.

What is the number? _____

5. I am thinking of a number.

It is less than 80.

It is greater than 70.

You say it when you count by 2s.

It has a 4 in the ones place.

What is the number? _____

6. I am thinking of a number.

It is less than 10.

It is odd.

It is greater than 7.

What is the number? _____

7. I am thinking of a number.

It is greater than 50.

It is less than 60.

It has a 3 in the ones place.

What is the number? _____

MIND-BENDER MATH

10 minutes

NUMBER RIDDLES

Activity
10

Directions

Use the hundreds chart to solve each riddle.

1	2	3	4	5	6	7	8	9	10
11	12	13	14	15	16	17	18	19	20
21	22	23	24	25	26	27	28	29	30
31	32	33	34	35	36	37	38	39	40
41	42	43	44	45	46	47	48	49	50
51	52	53	54	55	56	57	58	59	60
61	62	63	64	65	66	67	68	69	70
71	72	73	74	75	76	77	78	79	80
81	82	83	84	85	86	87	88	89	90
91	92	93	94	95	96	97	98	99	100

MIND-BENDER MATH

Riddle 1

1. I am larger than 30 and less than 50.
2. I am an even number.
3. When you count by 10s you say my name.
   What number am I? _____

Riddle 3

1. I am less than 40 but larger than 10.
2. I have two numbers that are the same. My two numbers added together equal 4.
   What number am I? _____

Riddle 2

1. I am larger than 50 and less than 100.
2. I have a 5 in the ones place.
3. I have a number smaller than 6 in the tens place.
   What number am I? _____

Riddle 4

1. I have a 2 as one of my numbers.
2. Counting by 10s you say my name.
   What number am I? _____

10
minutes

FIND THE PAIR

Directions

Color the two pictures in each box that are the same.

1.

4.

2.

5.

3.

6.

BEYOND BRAINY

5 minutes

NAME _____   DATE _____

ALPHABET MAZE

Activity 72

Directions

Follow the alphabet through the maze to get the children to school.

Start

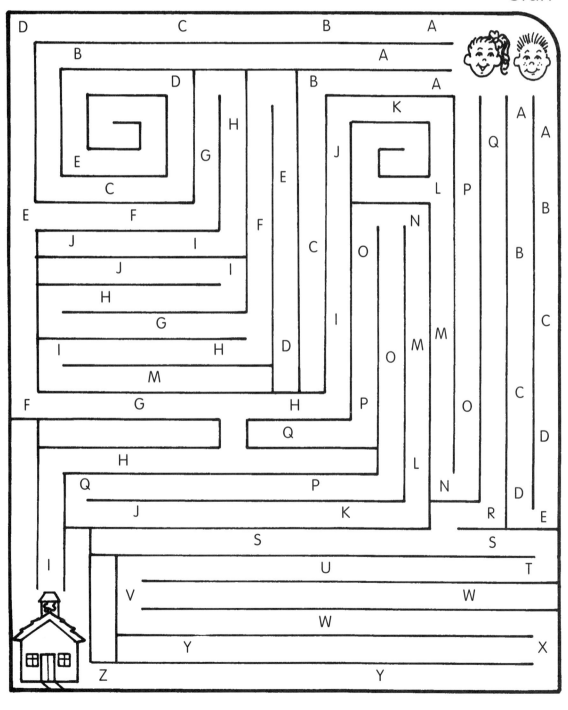

BEYOND BRAINY

5 minutes

COPY CATS

Activity
13

Directions

Copy the lines on the left onto the dots on the right.

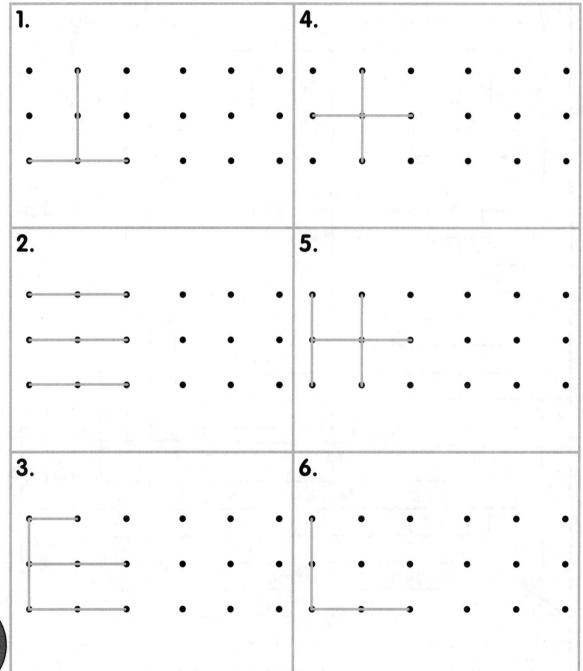

1.

2.

3.

4.

5.

6.

5 minutes

WHAT COMES NEXT?

Activity
74

Directions

Color the first three shapes, and then the shape that comes next in the pattern. Use a different color for each row.

1.

2.

3.

4.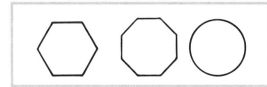

5.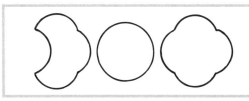

5
minutes

BEYOND BRAINY

OUT OF PLACE

Activity
75

Directions

Circle the picture in each row that is different from the others.

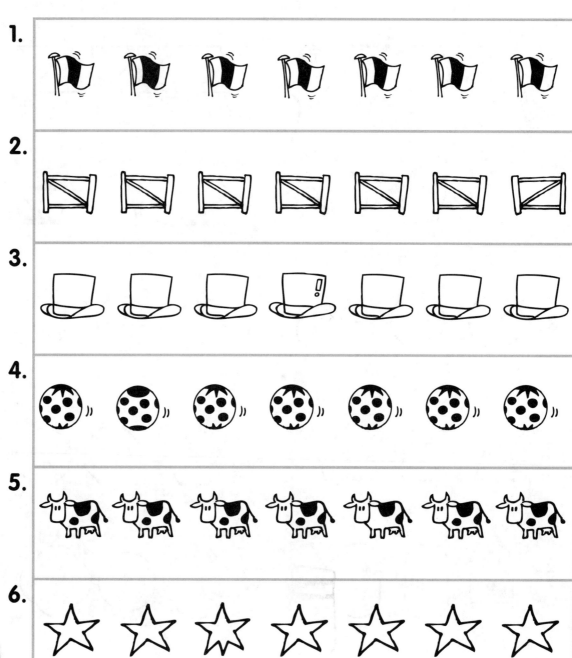

BEYOND **B**RAINY

5
minutes

SOCK MATCH

Activity
76

Directions

Color the socks that make a pair. Color each pair a different color.

BEYOND BRAINY

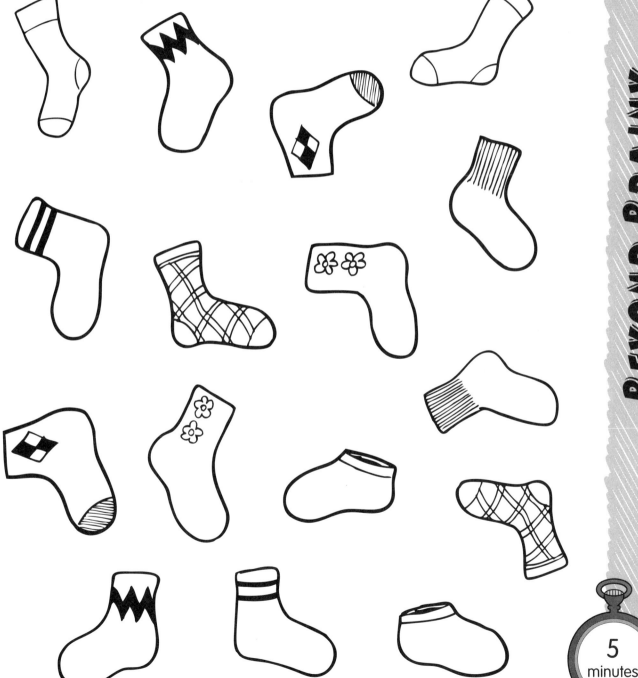

5 minutes

HALF A PICTURE

Activity
11

Directions

Draw in the missing part of the picture using the grid to help you. Color in the whole picture.

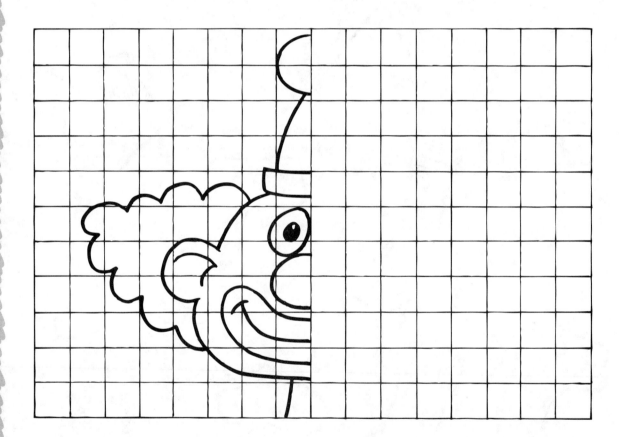

BEYOND BRAINY

10
minutes

CAREFUL COLOR

Directions

Color this design using only three colors and making sure that no shapes of the same color touch each other.

BEYOND BRAINY

10 minutes

SCRAMBLED COLORS

Activity 79

Directions

Unscramble the color words. Then find and circle them in the word search below. Words can be found going across, down, backwards, or upside-down.

BEYOND BRAINY

1. der = _____

2. lewylo = _____

3. nerge = _____

4. lcakb = _____

5. ubel = _____

6. lurppe = _____

7. ageorn = _____

8. thiwe = _____

N	E	E	R	G	P	C
J	U	A	B	L	U	W
B	L	A	C	K	R	O
C	B	R	E	D	P	L
E	T	I	H	W	L	L
O	R	A	N	G	E	E
R	D	S	T	O	H	Y

10 minutes

ADD ON

Activity
80

Directions

Add the missing pieces to the second picture in each pair to finish the pictures.

1.

4.

2.

5.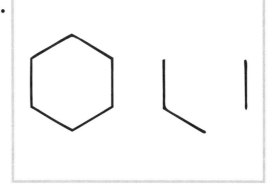

3.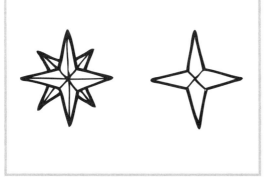

6.

5 minutes

BEYOND BRAINY

Inside and Outside

Directions

Color **red** those things you would find **inside** your home. Color **yellow** those things you would find **outside** your home.

TRICKY SHAPES

Activity
82

Directions

Count the number of each shape in the design below.

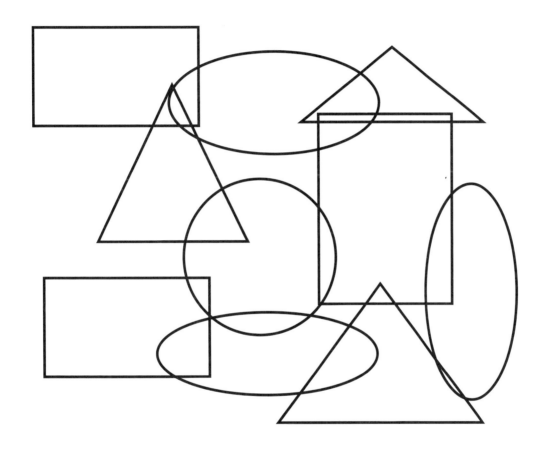

BEYOND BRAINY

How many?

◯ circles = _____   △ triangles = _____

◯ ovals = _____   ▯ rectangles = _____

5 minutes

CONNECT THE DOTS

Directions

Connect the dots from 1 to 50 to see the picture.

BEYOND BRAINY

5 minutes

THE SAME

Activity
84

Directions

Look at the shapes in the box. Color each one a different color. Now find its partner outside the box and color it to match.

BEYOND BRAINY

5 minutes

BOB'S KITE

Directions

Bob lost his kite. Can you help him find it?
Circle the correct kite. Here are facts
about Bob's kite:

> ✓ It does not have flowers on it.
>
> ✓ It does not have bows on it.
>
> ✓ It has stripes on it.

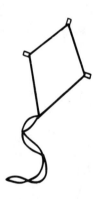  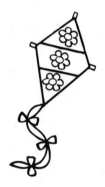 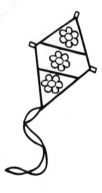

   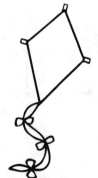

BEYOND BRAINY

5 minutes

HIDDEN PICTURES

Activity
86

Directions

There is a list of hidden pictures at the bottom of the page. Circle or color each object in the picture that you find from the list. Can you find all ten?

BEYOND BRAINY

sandwich	grapes	pear	bread	hamburger
chicken leg	soda can	carrot	apple	banana

10 minutes

MAP MADNESS

Activity **87**

Directions

Do you see Frank? He is lost! Follow the map directions to get him back on track. Mark his ending spot with an **X**.

Map Directions:

1. ⬆ Go north on Oak St.

2. ⬅ Go west on 3rd St.

3. END End at the corner of Maple St.

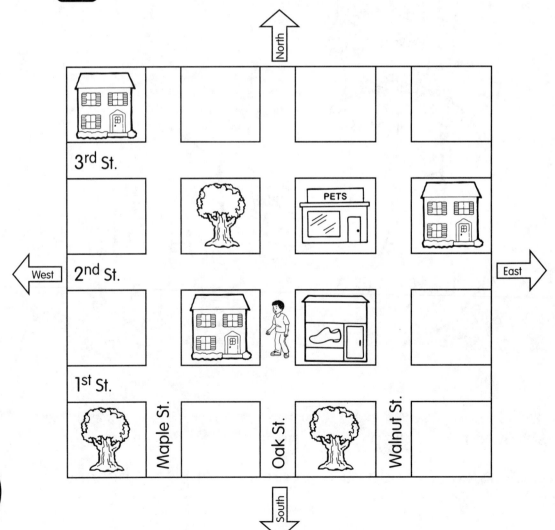

COLOR IN

Directions

A beautiful scene is hidden in the shapes below. Color the shapes marked: BL in blue, O in orange, P in pink, G in light green, DG in dark green, Y in yellow, and BR in brown.

10 minutes

MATCH UP

Activity
89

Directions

Look at the picture pairs below. If the two pictures are the same, color them red. If they are different, color one red and one blue.

1.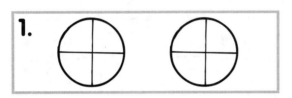

2.

3.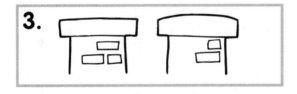

4.

5.

6.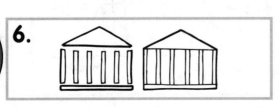

7.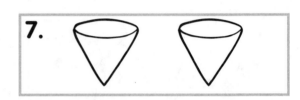

8.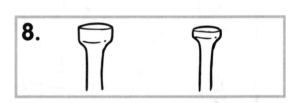

9.

10.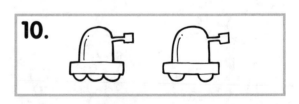

11.

12.

10 minutes

BEYOND BRAINY

CROSSWORD PUZZLER

Activity 90

Directions

Complete the crossword puzzle using the clues below to help you.

Beyond Brainy

1.					2.		3.			
				4.						
		5.							

Across

1. what birds do with their wings in the air
3. what you do to watermelon seeds
4. something people set to catch animals
5. what you do at the end of a performance to show how much you enjoyed it

Down

1. what you don't want to do in the water: a belly _____
2. another word for vacation
3. something black on a Dalmatian dog

10 minutes

TIME TO DRAW

Directions

Help Timmy find his way to the cat drawing.

Start

Finish

BEYOND BRAINY

5 minutes

94

CHANGE IT UP

Activity
92

Directions

Change one letter at a time to get from the top word to the bottom word. Each row must make a real word.

Example:

p	a	n
p	**i**	n
p	i	**g**
b	i	g

BEYOND BRAINY

1.

h	a	t
b	e	d

2.

m	o	p
c	a	r

10 minutes

COLOR INS

Directions

Using any colors, shade each of these designs exactly the same as the smaller designs below.

 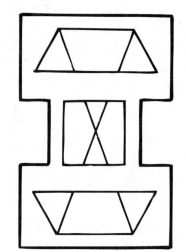 

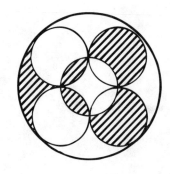 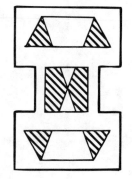 

BEYOND BRAINY

10 minutes

READ AND DRAW

Directions

1. Draw a dog under the tree.
2. Draw five sheep in the far field.
3. Draw two birds in the tree.
4. Draw two eggs in the bird's nest.
5. Draw someone flying a kite.

Beyond Brainy

10 minutes

WHOSE BALL?

BEYOND BRAINY

Directions

Four balls were found in the neighborhood. Mr. Smith wants to return them. Can you help him find the owners? Use the clues below to help you. Write the answers on the lines below.

Clues

Glenn loves to play a team game with a goalie.
Fred uses a bat to hit his ball.
Jeff uses his ball to shoot hoops.
Steve knocks things down with his ball.

baseball

soccer ball

bowling ball

basketball

1. Glenn owns the _____ .

2. Fred owns the _____ .

3. Jeff owns the _____ .

4. Steve owns the _____ .

10 minutes

Math Triangles

Activity
96

Directions

In the first triangle, fill in the squares so that the sum of each side of the triangle is seven. In the second triangle, make each side equal ten.

1. each side = 7

```
        3
   □         □
□        4        2
```

BEYOND BRAINY

---

2. each side = 10

```
        5
   □         2
□        4        □
```

10
minutes

HIDDEN ANIMALS

Activity

97

Directions

Hidden in each sentence are two animal names. Can you find them? Circle them and write the names on the lines.

Example: Help   igloos! ➜ pig

1. Can't Jill go at all?   _____

2. Did Kelli once use a lasso?   _____

3. Alec owned ogres.   _____

4. Be earlier at once!   _____

5. She ate grapes and a bowl of popcorn.

_____

10 minutes

BEYOND BRAINY

PAY FOR IT

Activity
98

Directions

Color in the coins that could be used to pay for each item. (There may be more than one combination of coins that will work.)

1. 5¢

2. 20¢

3. 27¢

4. 13¢

5. 32¢

6. 7¢

7. 52¢

8. 17¢

BEYOND BRAINY

10 minutes

VISITING FRIENDS

Activity
99

Directions

Find out who lives in the following houses by answering each question below.

Maria

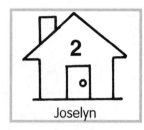
Joselyn

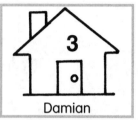
Damian

North
West — East
South

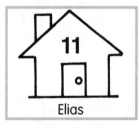
Elias

Selina

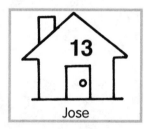
Jose

Derikka

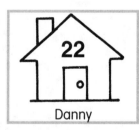
Danny

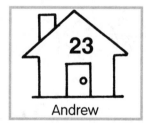
Andrew

BEYOND BRAINY

1. The house north of Selina's? _____

2. The house south of Elias'? _____

3. The house west of Selina's?_____

4. The house east of Joselyn's? _____

5. The house south of Damian's? _____

6. The house south of Joselyn's? _____

10 minutes

WHAT'S THE SAME?

Activity
100

Directions

The words in each column below have something in common. Can you find out what it is?

Column 1	Column 2	Column 3	Column 4	Column 5
with	would	rats	little	she
them	you	star	his	he
path	out	arts	like	we
they	your	tars	said	see

What's the same in …

Column 1? _____

Column 2? _____

Column 3? _____

Column 4? _____

Column 5? _____

BEYOND BRAINY

10
minutes

NAME _____   DATE _____

WHO ATE WHAT?

Directions

Jack, Maria, and Tim ate lunch. Read each clue. Then mark the chart to see who ate what. Draw an **X** in the box to show a food that was not eaten. Draw a ✓ in the box to show what someone ate.

Clues:

✓ Tim did not eat a sandwich.

✓ Maria did not eat a hot dog.

✓ Jack had the salad.

	Sandwich	Hot Dog	Salad
Jack			
Maria			
Tim			

1. What did Jack eat for lunch?_____

2. What did Maria eat for lunch? _____

10 minutes

3. What did Tim eat for lunch? _____

BEYOND BRAINY

Answer Key

Activity 1
1. sun
2. pig
3. hat
4. pen
5. dog

Activity 2
1. clown
2. crown
3. snow
4. bowl
5. town

Activity 3
1. sail
2. rain
3. train
4. chain
5. mail
6. tail
7. snail
8. brain

Activity 4
1. pad
2. cup
3. jam
4. beg
5. can
6. let

Activity 5
1. fox
2. box
3. top
4. mat
5. fan
6. mop

Activity 6
1. map; pan
2. fox; rock
3. bed; bell
4. hill; kick

Activity 7
1. gold
2. star
3. wing
4. drum
5. ship
6. flag
7. wheel
8. broom

Activity 8
1. fox
2. bed
3. cup
4. bat

Activity 9
1. kick
2. van
3. log
4. wig
5. web
6. swim
7. cup
8. well

Activity 10
1. snow
2. meat
3. flag
4. cart
5. gold
6. coat
7. four
8. star

Activity 11
1. moon
2. queen
3. spoon
4. broom
5. tooth
6. feet
7. sleep
8. deer
9. seeds

Activity 12
1. ball
2. nest
3. ship
4. star
5. lock
6. drum

Activity 13
1. mat
2. rain
3. heel
4. cave
5. room
6. ring

ANSWER KEY (cont.)

Activity 14
1. ship
2. snake
3. shoe
4. snow
5. flower
6. truck
7. swim
8. brick
9. snail

Activity 15
1. rat
2. arm
3. pan
4. saw
5. ten
6. ant

Activity 16
Toys (red): top, ball, doll, kite
Animals (blue): zebra, horse, tiger, pig, mouse
Birds (yellow): eagle, hawk, swan, crow, duck
Toy and Animal (green): bat

Activity 17
A BIG DOG BIT ME.

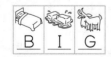

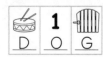

Activity 18
1. man
2. hat
3. ten
4. net
5. pig
6. pin
7. mop
8. bug

Activity 19
Check drawings for accuracy.

Activity 20

c	o	w	p	i	g	
h	o	r	s	e	d	
b	e	a	r	f	o	
t	i	g	e	r	g	
r	a	b	b	i	t	

1. bear
2. cow
3. dog
4. horse
5. pig
6. rabbit
7. tiger

Activity 21
1. baby
2. bath
3. dash
4. dress
5. foot
6. football
7. ice
8. igloo
9. mirror
10. monkey
11. wombat
12. wooly

Activity 22
1. pool
2. cake
3. milk
4. card
5. goat
6. wing
7. pear
8. rain
9. duck

Activity 23
1. cat, can, cap, car
2. bat, bin, bag, bun

Activity 24
1. sun
2. cat
3. leg
4. big
5. fry

Activity 25
Answers will vary.

Activity 26
1. hat
2. dog
3. sun
4. get
5. sad
6. man
7. dig
8. ten

Answer Key (cont.)

Activity 27
Short A: cab, plan, snap
Short E: yet, fed, best
Short I: stick, rip, swim
Short O: dock, fog, spot
Short U: plug, cut, stub
Long A: take, grape, blame
Long E: leap, green, eel
Long I: bride, line, like
Long O: boat, woke, note
Long U: mule, juice, cute

Activity 28
Beginning consonant words:
duck, fall, milk, nut, play, sack
Middle consonant words:
ladder, gift, camel, runt,
apple, vest
Final consonant words: lid,
leaf, gum, rain, cup, bus

Activity 29
1. He cut up the log.
2. A bug on the jug.
3. She runs in the mud.
4. A cat sits on Mom.

Activity 30
Answers will vary.

Activity 31
1. milk
2. tent
3. cry
4. monkey
5. rabbit
6. ran

Activity 32
1. bee
2. banana
3. rose
4. zebra
5. carrot

Activity 33
1. The dog is so cute.
2. She just had eight
   puppies.
3. There were two black
   puppies.
4. Five puppies were
   brown.
5. What was the color of
   the last one?

Activity 34
Answers will vary.

Activity 35
Answers will vary.

Activity 36
10 of each object should be
colored.

Activity 37
There are 12 squares.

Activity 38
1st ball = orange
2nd ball = brown
3rd ball = yellow
4th ball = green
5th ball = pink
6th ball = red

Activity 39
Row 1: 4 more balls should
       be drawn.
Row 2: 6 more dogs should
       be drawn.
Row 3: 5 more pears should
       be drawn.
Row 4: 6 more cakes should
       be drawn.
Row 5: 3 more ladybugs
       should be drawn.

Activity 40

Activity 41
1. triangle
2. hexagon
3. circle
4. pentagon
5. rectangle
6. square

Activity 42
Shapes should be colored
as indicated.

Answer Key (cont.)

Activity 43

2 birds
4 sheep
2 pigs
1 cat
3 dogs
9 trees
5 flowers
5 people
6 ducks

Activity 44

Green leaves (right):

$3 + 3 = 6$
$7 + 5 = 12$
$6 + 4 = 10$
$4 + 4 = 8$
$6 + 7 = 13$
$3 + 9 = 12$
$5 + 3 = 8$

Brown leaves (wrong):

$8 + 4 = 13$
$12 + 3 = 10$
$8 + 8 = 12$

Activity 45

Blue balloons (odd):

$3 + 2 = 5$
$4 + 3 = 7$
$7 + 2 = 9$
$6 + 3 = 9$
$2 + 5 = 7$

Red balloons (even):

$1 + 9 = 10$
$4 + 4 = 8$
$4 + 2 = 6$
$6 + 2 = 8$

Activity 46

Fish that should be colored:

$6 + 4 = 10$
$9 + 3 = 12$
$10 - 4 = 6$
$12 - 3 = 9$
$8 - 5 = 3$
$14 - 4 = 10$

Activity 47

1.
2.
3.
4.
5.

Activity 48

Triangles = 5
Rectangles = 3
Squares = 2
Circles = 6

Activity 49

1. 9, 10
2. 18, 20
3. 17, 19
4. 5, 5
5. 1, 0
6. 45, 50
7. 25, 28
8. 90, 100
9. 2, 0
10. 0, 5

Activity 50

Matching socks:

$10 + 2$ and $6 + 6$
$8 + 3$ and $6 + 5$
$5 + 5$ and $6 + 4$
$2 + 5$ and $4 + 3$
$8 + 5$ and $6 + 7$
$4 + 2$ and $1 + 5$

Activity 51

James' fish (odd, red):

$8 + 5 = 13$
$5 + 4 = 9$
$12 - 3 = 9$
$7 - 2 = 5$
$7 + 2 = 9$

Jackie's fish (even, blue):

$3 + 5 = 8$
$10 - 4 = 6$
$12 - 6 = 6$
$9 + 3 = 12$
$11 - 3 = 8$

Activity 52

1. $3 + 2 = 5$
2. $6 + 1 = 7$
3. $5 + 3 = 8$
4. $4 + 2 = 6$
5. $3 + 0 = 3$
6. $4 + 4 = 8$

Activity 53

1. 3, 5
2. 6, 6
3. 2, 4
4. 12, 8
5. 4, 6
6. 8, 8

Answer Key (cont.)

Activity 54

1. 3 + 5; 7 + 1; 6 + 2
2. 2 + 2; 4 + 0; 3 + 1; 0 + 4
3. 6 + 0; 4 + 2; 3 + 3; 5 + 1
4. 2 + 0; 1 + 1; 0 + 2
5. 3 + 6; 1 + 8; 9 + 0
6. 3 + 0; 2 + 1; 0 + 3; 1 + 2
7. 6 + 1; 2 + 5; 4 + 3; 7 + 0
8. 5 + 0; 3 + 2; 1 + 4; 2 + 3

Activity 55

1. 5
2. 5
3. 9
4. 6
5. 8
6. 5

Activity 56

1. 6
2. 8
3. 14
4. 14
5. 11
6. 11
7. 11
8. 19
9. 5
10. 14
11. 10

Activity 57

Across
1. fourteen
2. seventeen
3. twelve
4. eighteen

Down
3. twenty
5. thirteen
6. fifteen
7. ten
8. eleven
9. nineteen
10. sixteen

Activity 58

1. 1
2. 5
3. 4
4. 3
5. 2
6. 10
7. 7
8. 0
9. 8
10. 6

TO GET TO THE OTHER SLIDE

Activity 59

1. 39
2. 75
3. 98
4. 49
5. 90
6. 22
7. 78
8. 29
9. 84
10. 56

Activity 60

1. 5 − 2 = 3
2. 6 − 4 = 2
3. 4 − 1 = 3
4. 7 − 6 = 1
5. 5 − 5 = 0
6. 6 − 3 = 3

Activity 61

1. D
2. C
3. E
4. A
5. F
6. B

Activity 62

1. 5
2. 11
3. 8
4. 9
5. 10
6. 9
7. 12
8. 13
9. 6
10. 7
11. 9
12. 12

If they lived by the BAY, they would be called BAGELS.

ANSWER KEY (cont.)

Activity 63
1. 6
2. 8
3. 6
4. 6
5. 5
6. 6
7. 3
8. 4
9. 5
10. 8
11. 5
12. 7
13. 3
14. 4
15. 4
16. 4
17. 3
18. 7
19. 8
20. 8

Activity 64
1. +
2. =
3. −
4. +
5. +
6. =
7. −
8. =
9. +
10. −
11. −
12. +

Activity 65
1. 0, 3, 4, 1, 2, 5, 5, 0, 5
   SAY CHEESE!
2. 4, 1, 2, 5, 0, 3, 4, 4
   LET'S ROLL!

Activity 66
4, 6, 3, 7, 6, 4, 5, 9, 10, 8, 5

Activity 67
1. <
2. >
3. >
4. >
5. =
6. >
7. <
8. =
9. >
10. <
11. <
12. >
13. <
14. <
15. >

Activity 68
1. 43, 41, 49
2. 19, 79, 9, 29
3. 25
4. 60, 30
5. 7, 8, 2
6. 100
7. 40, 90, 100
8. 5, 30, 50, 65

Activity 69
1. 22
2. 35
3. 72
4. 10
5. 74
6. 9
7. 53

Activity 70
1. 40
2. 55
3. 22
4. 20

Activity 71
1.   4.

2.    5.

3.    6.

Activity 72

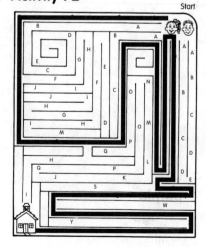

ANSWER KEY (cont.)

Activity 73

Check drawings for accuracy.

Activity 74

1. ⊠
2. ⬠ (shaded pentagon)
3. (circle with notch)
4. ⬡ (hexagon)
5. (rounded shape)

Activity 75

1. Circle the 2nd picture.
2. Circle the 7th picture.
3. Circle the 4th picture.
4. Circle the 2nd picture.
5. Circle the 5th picture.
6. Circle the 3rd picture.

Activity 76

Check coloring for accuracy.

Activity 77

Check drawing for accuracy.

Activity 78

Check coloring for accuracy.

Activity 79

1. red
2. yellow
3. green
4. black
5. blue
6. purple
7. orange
8. white

Activity 79 *(cont.)*

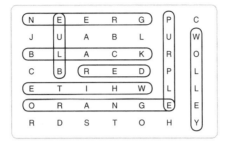

Activity 80

Check drawings for accuracy.

Activity 81

Red: bed, teapot, TV, bathtub

Yellow: hose, tree, pool, shovel

Activity 82

Circles = 1
Ovals = 3
Triangles = 3
Rectangles = 3

Activity 83

Activity 84

Check coloring for accuracy.

Activity 85

Bob's kite only has stripes on it.

Activity 86

Activity 87

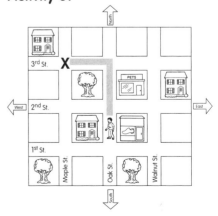

ANSWER KEY (cont.)

Activity 88
Check coloring for accuracy.

Activity 89
1. same
2. different
3. different
4. same
5. same
6. different
7. same
8. different
9. same
10. different
11. different
12. same

Activity 90
Across
1. flap
3. spit
4. trap
5. clap
Down
1. flop
2. trip
3. spot

Activity 91

Activity 92
1. bat, bet or had, bad
2. cop, cap

Activity 93
Check coloring for accuracy.

Activity 94
Check drawings for accuracy.

Activity 95
1. soccer ball
2. baseball
3. basketball
4. bowling ball

Activity 96

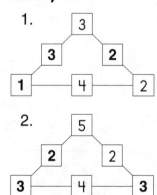

Activity 97
1. ant, goat
2. lion, seal
3. cow, dog
4. bee, rat
5. ape, owl

Activity 98
Answers will vary.

Activity 99
1. Joselyn
2. Derikka
3. Elias
4. Damian
5. Jose
6. Selina

Activity 100
Column 1: th
Column 2: ou
Column 3: same letters
Column 4: letter i
Column 5: long *E* sound

Activity 101
1. Jack ate the salad.
2. Maria ate the sandwich.
3. Tim ate the hot dog.